God Is Always With You

A Promise Journal

...inspired by life

Ever Present

Do you believe that God is near? He wants you to.
He wants you to know that He is in the midst of your
world. Wherever you are as you read these words,
He is present. In your car. On the plane. In your
office, your bedroom, your den. He's near.
And He is more than near. He is active.

MAX LUCADO

God may be invisible, but He's in touch. You
may not be able to see Him, but He is in control.
And that includes you—your circumstances.
That includes what you've just lost. That includes
what you've just gained. That includes
all of life—past, present, future.

CHARLES R. SWINDOLL

There's not a tint that paints the rose
Or decks the lily fair,
Or marks the humblest flower that grows,
But God has placed it there....
There's not a place on earth's vast round,
In ocean's deep or air,
Where love and beauty are not found,
For God is everywhere.

God is our refuge and strength, an ever-present help in trouble.
Therefore we will not fear.

PSALM 46:1–2 NIV

Shepherd and Guardian

Jesus said... "I am the good shepherd.
The good shepherd lays down his life for the sheep.
The hired hand is not the shepherd and does not own the sheep.
So when he sees the wolf coming,
he abandons the sheep and runs away....

"I am the good shepherd; I know my sheep
and my sheep know me—just as the Father knows me
and I know the Father—and I lay down my life for the sheep."

JOHN 10:7, 11–12, 14–15 NIV

He will feed his flock like a shepherd.
He will carry the lambs in his arms,
holding them close to his heart.

ISAIAH 40:11 NLT

All we like sheep have gone astray;
we have turned every one to his own way;
and the LORD hath laid on him the iniquity of us all.

ISAIAH 53:6 KJV

You were continually straying like sheep,
but now you have returned to the Shepherd
and Guardian of your souls.

1 PETER 2:25 NASB

Genuine love sees faces, not a mass:
the Good Shepherd calls His own sheep by name.

GEORGE A. BUTTRICK

....

....

....

....

....

....

....

....

....

....

....

....

....

Accessible

The wonder of our Lord is that He is so accessible to us
in the common things of our lives: the cup of water...
breaking of the bread...welcoming children into our arms...
fellowship over a meal...giving thanks. A simple attitude of caring,
listening, and lovingly telling the truth.

NANCIE CARMICHAEL

God's friendship is the unexpected joy we find
when we reach for His outstretched hand.

JANET L. SMITH

The sunshine dancing on the water, the lulling sound
of waves rolling into the shore, the glittering stars against
the night sky—all God's light, His warmth, His majesty—
our Father of light reaching out to us,
drawing each of us closer to Himself.

WENDY MOORE

Prayer is...an ever-available door by which
to come into God's presence.

DOUGLAS V. STEERE

If God is here for us and not elsewhere,
then in fact *this place* is holy and *this moment* is sacred.

ISABEL ANDERS

For through Him we both have access
by one Spirit to the Father.

EPHESIANS 2:18 NKJV

The Grace of God

But God, being rich in mercy,
because of His great love with which He loved us,
even when we were dead in our transgressions,
made us alive together with Christ
(by grace you have been saved),
and raised us up with Him, and seated us with
Him in the heavenly places in Christ Jesus,
so that in the ages to come He might
show the surpassing riches of His grace
in kindness toward us in Christ Jesus.
For by grace you have been saved through faith;
and that not of yourselves, it is the gift of God;
not as a result of works, so that no one may boast.
For we are His workmanship, created in Christ Jesus
for good works, which God prepared beforehand
so that we would walk in them.

EPHESIANS 2:4–10 NASB

Let us come boldly to the throne of our gracious God.
There we will receive his mercy, and we will find grace
to help us when we need it most.

HEBREWS 4:16 NLT

Grace means that God already loves us as much
as an infinite God can possibly love.

PHILIP YANCEY

Expectant Reverence

God cares for the world He created,
from the rising of a nation to the falling of the sparrow.
Everything in the world lies under the watchful gaze
of His providential eyes, from the numbering of the days
of our life to the numbering of the hairs on our head.
When we look at the world from that perspective,
it produces within us a response of reverence.

KEN GIRE

God is within all things, but not included;
outside all things, but not excluded;
above all things, but not beyond their reach.

POPE GREGORY I

There is a unique kind of transparence about things and events.
The world is seen through, and no veil can conceal God
completely. So those who are [devout] are ever alert to see
behind the appearance of things a trace of the divine, and thus
their attitude toward life is one of expectant reverence.

ABRAHAM JOSHUA HESCHEL

Because God created the Natural—
invented it out of His love and artistry—
it demands our reverence.

C. S. LEWIS

For you who revere my name, the sun of righteousness
will rise with healing in its rays.

MALACHI 4:2 NIV

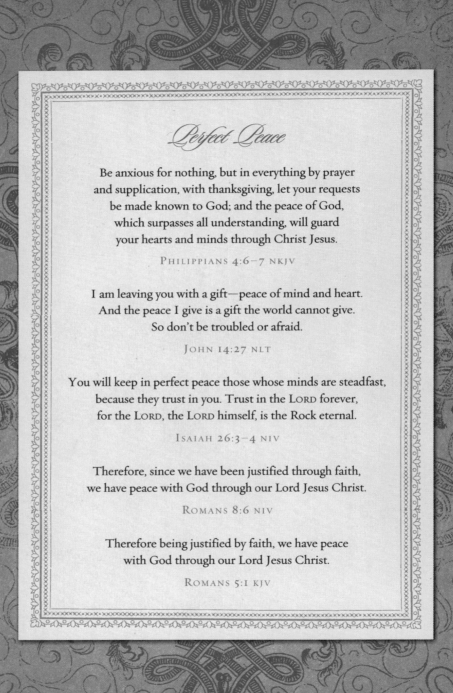

Perfect Peace

Be anxious for nothing, but in everything by prayer
and supplication, with thanksgiving, let your requests
be made known to God; and the peace of God,
which surpasses all understanding, will guard
your hearts and minds through Christ Jesus.

PHILIPPIANS 4:6–7 NKJV

I am leaving you with a gift—peace of mind and heart.
And the peace I give is a gift the world cannot give.
So don't be troubled or afraid.

JOHN 14:27 NLT

You will keep in perfect peace those whose minds are steadfast,
because they trust in you. Trust in the LORD forever,
for the LORD, the LORD himself, is the Rock eternal.

ISAIAH 26:3–4 NIV

Therefore, since we have been justified through faith,
we have peace with God through our Lord Jesus Christ.

ROMANS 8:6 NIV

Therefore being justified by faith, we have peace
with God through our Lord Jesus Christ.

ROMANS 5:1 KJV

The God of peace gives perfect peace to those
whose hearts are stayed upon Him.

CHARLES H. SPURGEON

....

....

....

....

....

....

....

....

....

....

....

....

....

....

The Goodness of God

All that is good, all that is true, all that is beautiful,
all that is beneficent, be it great or small, be it perfect
or fragmentary, natural as well as supernatural,
moral as well as material, comes from God.

CARDINAL JOHN HENRY NEWMAN

We walk without fear, full of hope and courage
and strength to do His will, waiting for
the endless good which He is always
giving as fast as He can get us able to take it in.

GEORGE MACDONALD

If you have a special need today, focus your full attention
on the goodness and greatness of your Father rather
than on the size of your need. Your need is so small
compared to His ability to meet it.

Open your mouth and taste, open your eyes and see—
how good God is. Blessed are you who run to him.
Worship God if you want the best;
worship opens doors to all his goodness.

PSALM 34:8–9 MSG

The goodness of God is infinitely more wonderful
than we will ever be able to comprehend.

A. W. TOZER

The Majesty of God

O Lord, our Lord,
how majestic is your name in all the earth!
You have set your glory above the heavens....
When I consider your heavens, the work of your fingers,
the moon and the stars, which you have set in place,
what is mankind that you are mindful of them,
human beings that you care for them?
You made them a little lower than the angels and
crowned them with glory and honor....
O Lord, our Lord,
how majestic is your name in all the earth!

PSALM 8:1, 3–5, 9 NIV

The Lord is king! He is robed in majesty.
Indeed, the Lord is robed in majesty and armed with strength.
The world stands firm and cannot be shaken.
Your throne, O Lord, has stood from time immemorial.
You yourself are from the everlasting past.

PSALM 93:1–2 NLT

All glory, majesty, power, and authority
are his before all time, and in the present,
and beyond all time! Amen.

JUDE 1:25 NLT

Let every kindred, every tribe, on this terrestrial ball,
To Him all majesty ascribe, and crown Him Lord of all.

EDWARD PERRONET

God Draws Near

We are of such value to God that He came to live among us...
and to guide us home. He will go to any length to seek us,
even to being lifted high upon the cross to draw us back
to Himself. We can only respond by loving God for His love.

CATHERINE OF SIENNA

When you are lonely I wish you love;
When you are down I wish you joy;
When you are troubled I wish you peace;
When things are complicated I wish you simple beauty;
When things are chaotic I wish you inner silence;
When things seem empty I wish you hope,
And the sweet sense of God's presence every passing day.

There are times when I draw near enough to touch Him.
Then I know that He has been there all the time.

GLORIA GAITHER

God still draws near to us in the ordinary, commonplace,
everyday experiences and places.... He comes in surprising ways.

HENRY GARIEPY

Whoso draws nigh to God
One step through doubtings dim,
God will advance a mile
In blazing light to him.

I have set the LORD always before me:
because he is at my right hand, I shall not be moved.

PSALM 16:8 KJV

....

....

....

....

....

....

....

....

....

....

....

....

....

....

The Power of God

Search high and low, scan skies and land,
you'll find nothing and no one quite like GOD.
The holy angels are in awe before him; he looms immense
and august over everyone around him. God of the Angel Armies,
who is like you, powerful and faithful from every angle?

PSALM 89:6–8 MSG

Yours, LORD, is the greatness and the power and the glory
and the majesty and the splendor, for everything in heaven
and earth is yours. Yours, LORD, is the kingdom;
you are exalted as head over all.

1 CHRONICLES 29:11 NIV

Ah, Sovereign LORD, you have made the heavens
and the earth by your great power and outstretched arm.
Nothing is too hard for you.

JEREMIAH 32:17 NIV

Now all glory to God, who is able to keep you
from falling away and will bring you with great joy
into his glorious presence without a single fault.
All glory to him who alone is God.

JUDE 1:24–25 NLT

Whatever the circumstances, whatever the call...
His strength will be your strength in your hour of need.

BILLY GRAHAM

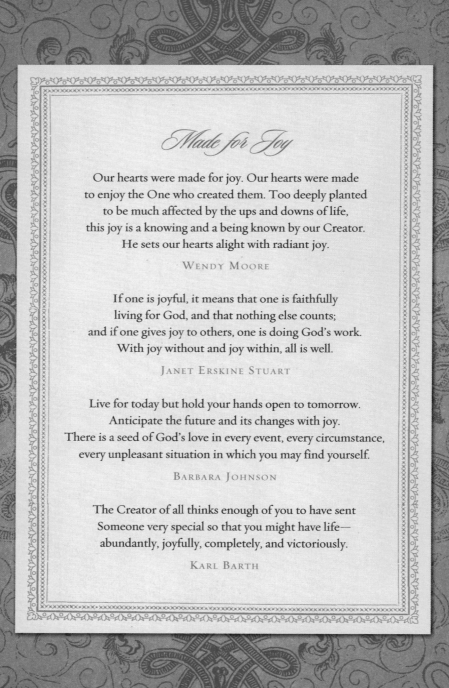

Made for Joy

Our hearts were made for joy. Our hearts were made
to enjoy the One who created them. Too deeply planted
to be much affected by the ups and downs of life,
this joy is a knowing and a being known by our Creator.
He sets our hearts alight with radiant joy.

WENDY MOORE

If one is joyful, it means that one is faithfully
living for God, and that nothing else counts;
and if one gives joy to others, one is doing God's work.
With joy without and joy within, all is well.

JANET ERSKINE STUART

Live for today but hold your hands open to tomorrow.
Anticipate the future and its changes with joy.
There is a seed of God's love in every event, every circumstance,
every unpleasant situation in which you may find yourself.

BARBARA JOHNSON

The Creator of all thinks enough of you to have sent
Someone very special so that you might have life—
abundantly, joyfully, completely, and victoriously.

KARL BARTH

The joy of the LORD is your strength.

NEHEMIAH 8:10 KJV

....

....

....

....

....

....

....

....

....

....

....

....

....

....

....

....

Love Like That

Watch what God does, and then you do it, like children
who learn proper behavior from their parents.
Mostly what God does is love you. Keep company with him
and learn a life of love. Observe how Christ loved us.
His love was not cautious but extravagant. He didn't love
in order to get something from us but to give
everything of himself to us. Love like that.

EPHESIANS 5:1–2 MSG

I pray that your love for each other
will overflow more and more, and that you will keep on
growing in knowledge and understanding.

PHILIPPIANS 1:9 NLT

Trust steadily in God, hope unswervingly, love extravagantly.
And the best of the three is love.

1 CORINTHIANS 13:13 MSG

If you have any encouragement from being
united with Christ, if any comfort from his love,
if any common sharing in the Spirit,
if any tenderness and compassion,
then make my joy complete by being like-minded,
having the same love, being one in spirit and of one mind.

PHILIPPIANS 2:1–2 NIV

Open your hearts to the love God instills.... God loves you tenderly.
What He gives you is not to be kept under lock and key, but to be shared.

MOTHER TERESA

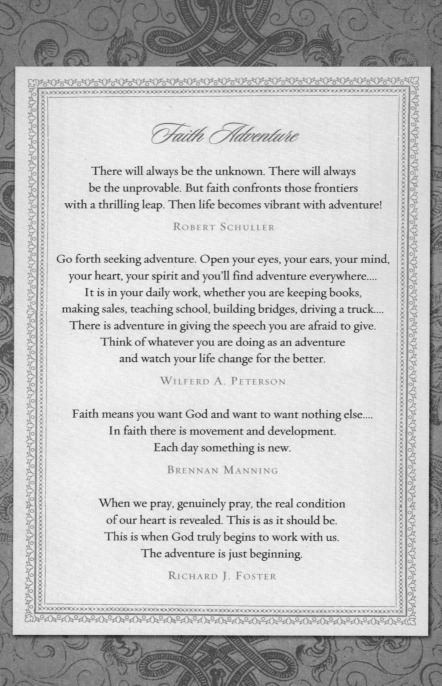

Faith Adventure

There will always be the unknown. There will always
be the unprovable. But faith confronts those frontiers
with a thrilling leap. Then life becomes vibrant with adventure!

ROBERT SCHULLER

Go forth seeking adventure. Open your eyes, your ears, your mind,
your heart, your spirit and you'll find adventure everywhere....
It is in your daily work, whether you are keeping books,
making sales, teaching school, building bridges, driving a truck....
There is adventure in giving the speech you are afraid to give.
Think of whatever you are doing as an adventure
and watch your life change for the better.

WILFERD A. PETERSON

Faith means you want God and want to want nothing else....
In faith there is movement and development.
Each day something is new.

BRENNAN MANNING

When we pray, genuinely pray, the real condition
of our heart is revealed. This is as it should be.
This is when God truly begins to work with us.
The adventure is just beginning.

RICHARD J. FOSTER

For with God all things are possible.

MARK 10:27 KJV

The Great Commission

Go therefore and make disciples of all the nations,
baptizing them in the name of the Father and the Son
and the Holy Spirit, teaching them to observe
all that I commanded you; and lo, I am with you always,
even to the end of the age.

MATTHEW 28:19–20 NASB

Do not let this one fact escape your notice, beloved,
that with the Lord one day is like a thousand years,
and a thousand years like one day. The Lord is not slow
about His promise, as some count slowness,
but is patient toward you, not wishing for any to perish
but for all to come to repentance.

2 PETER 3:8–9 NASB

My goal is that...they may have the full riches
of complete understanding, in order that they may know
the mystery of God, namely, Christ, in whom are hidden
all the treasures of wisdom and knowledge.

COLOSSIANS 2:2–3 NIV

For it is God who works in you to will and to act
in order to fulfill his good purpose.

PHILIPPIANS 2:13 NIV

*God has always used ordinary people to
carry out His extraordinary mission.*

....

....

....

....

....

....

....

....

....

....

....

....

....

....

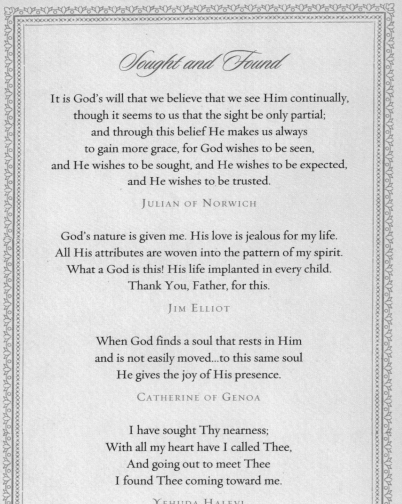

Sought and Found

It is God's will that we believe that we see Him continually,
though it seems to us that the sight be only partial;
and through this belief He makes us always
to gain more grace, for God wishes to be seen,
and He wishes to be sought, and He wishes to be expected,
and He wishes to be trusted.

JULIAN OF NORWICH

God's nature is given me. His love is jealous for my life.
All His attributes are woven into the pattern of my spirit.
What a God is this! His life implanted in every child.
Thank You, Father, for this.

JIM ELLIOT

When God finds a soul that rests in Him
and is not easily moved...to this same soul
He gives the joy of His presence.

CATHERINE OF GENOA

I have sought Thy nearness;
With all my heart have I called Thee,
And going out to meet Thee
I found Thee coming toward me.

YEHUDA HALEVI

Seek the Lord your God, and you will find him
if you seek him with all your heart and with all your soul.

DEUTERONOMY 4:29 NIV

....

....

....

....

....

....

....

....

....

....

....

....

....

....

....

God's Care

The LORD is my shepherd; I shall not want.
He maketh me to lie down in green pastures:
he leadeth me beside the still waters.
He restoreth my soul:
he leadeth me in the paths of
righteousness for his name's sake.
Yea, though I walk through the valley
of the shadow of death, I will fear no evil:
for thou art with me; thy rod and thy staff
they comfort me. Thou preparest a table
before me in the presence of mine enemies:
thou anointest my head with oil; my cup
runneth over. Surely goodness and mercy
shall follow me all the days of my life: and I will
dwell in the house of the LORD for ever.

PSALM 23:1–6 KJV

The Sovereign LORD says: I myself will search
and find my sheep. I will be like a shepherd looking
for his scattered flock. I will find my sheep and rescue them
from all the places where they were scattered
on that dark and cloudy day.

EZEKIEL 34:11–12 NLT

God never abandons anyone on whom He has set His love;
nor does Christ, the good shepherd, ever lose track of His sheep.

J. I. PACKER

....

....

....

....

....

....

....

....

....

....

....

....

....

....

The Road Ahead

My Lord God, I have no idea where I am going. I do not
see the road ahead of me. I cannot know for certain
where it will end.... But I believe that the desire to please You
does in fact please You. And I hope I have that desire in all that
I am doing. I hope that I will never do anything apart
from that desire. And I know that if I do this, You will lead me
by the right road though I may know nothing about it.

Therefore will I trust You always though
I may seem to be lost and in the shadow of death.
I will not fear, for You are ever with me.
And You will never leave me to face my perils alone.

THOMAS MERTON

God came to us because [He] wanted to join us on the road,
to listen to our story, and to help us realize that we
are not walking in circles but moving toward
the house of peace and joy.

HENRI J. M. NOUWEN

I would rather walk with God in the dark
than go alone in the light.

MARY GARDINER BRAINARD

I am always with you;
you hold me by my right hand.

PSALM 73:23 NIV

....

....

....

....

....

....

....

....

....

....

....

....

....

....

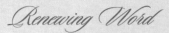

Renewing Word

You're my place of quiet retreat; I wait for your Word
to renew me.... Therefore I lovingly
embrace everything you say.

PSALM 119:114, 119 MSG

You have dealt well with Your servant, O LORD, according
to Your word. Teach me good discernment and knowledge,
for I believe in Your commandments. Before I was afflicted
I went astray, but now I keep Your word.
You are good and do good; teach me Your statutes.

PSALM 119:65–68 NASB

The everlasting God, the LORD...
Neither faints nor is weary.
His understanding is unsearchable.
He gives power to the weak,
And to those who have no might He increases strength.
Even the youths shall faint and be weary,
And the young men shall utterly fall,
But those who wait on the LORD
Shall renew their strength;
They shall mount up with wings like eagles,
They shall run and not be weary,
They shall walk and not faint.

ISAIAH 40:28–31 NKJV

Be still, and in the quiet moments, listen to the voice of your heavenly Father.
His words can renew your spirit...no one knows you and your needs like He does.

JANET L. SMITH

....

....

....

....

....

....

....

....

....

....

....

....

....

....

Grace Revealed

Look deep within yourself and recognize what brings life
and grace into your heart. It is this that can be shared
with those around you. You are loved by God.
This is an inspiration to love.

CHRISTOPHER DE VINCK

All God's glory and beauty come from within, and there
He delights to dwell. His visits there are frequent,
His conversation sweet, His comforts refreshing,
His peace passing all understanding.

THOMAS À KEMPIS

The Lord's chief desire is to reveal Himself to you and,
in order for Him to do that, He gives you abundant grace.
The Lord gives you the experience of enjoying His presence.
He touches you, and His touch is so delightful that,
more than ever, you are drawn inwardly to Him.

MADAME JEANNE GUYON

Brightness of my Father's glory,
Sunshine of my Father's face,
Let thy glory e'er shine on me,
Fill me with Thy grace.

JEAN SOPHIA PIGOTT

*Set your hope fully on the grace to be brought you
when Jesus Christ is revealed.*

1 PETER 1:13 NIV

....

....

....

....

....

....

....

....

....

....

....

....

....

Restoration

The Spirit of the Sovereign LORD is on me,
because the LORD has anointed me to proclaim
good news to the poor. He has sent me
to bind up the brokenhearted, to proclaim
freedom for the captives and release
from darkness for the prisoners, to proclaim
the year of the LORD's favor and the day
of vengeance of our God, to comfort all who mourn,
and provide for those who grieve in Zion—
to bestow on them a crown of beauty instead of ashes,
the oil of gladness instead of mourning,
and a garment of praise instead of a spirit of despair.
They will be called oaks of righteousness,
a planting of the LORD
for the display of his splendor.

ISAIAH 61:1–3 NIV

The law of the LORD is perfect, restoring the soul;
The testimony of the LORD is sure, making wise the simple.
The precepts of the LORD are right, rejoicing the heart;
The commandment of the LORD is pure, enlightening the eyes.
The fear of the LORD is clean, enduring forever.

PSALM 19:7–9 NASB

*The Lord promises to bind up the brokenhearted, to give relief
and full deliverance to those whose spirits have been weighed down.*

CHARLES R. SWINDOLL

For Himself

Although it be good to think upon the kindness of God,
and to love Him and worship Him for it; yet it is far better
to gaze upon the pure essence of Him and to love Him
and worship Him for Himself.

The first time God gave Himself a name in the Bible,
He called Himself the "I Am." He is the one who is
from eternity to eternity. He is the one who never changes.
He is the one who calls you by name
and numbers the hairs on your head.

JOANIE GARBORG

We desire many things, and God offers us only one thing.
He can offer us only one thing—Himself.
He has nothing else to give. There is nothing else to give.

PETER KREEFT

The reason for loving God is God Himself,
and the measure in which we should love Him
is to love Him without measure.

BERNARD OF CLAIRVAUX

God bless you and utterly satisfy your heart...with Himself.

AMY CARMICHAEL

The LORD alone shall be exalted.

ISAIAH 2:11 KJV

....

....

....

....

....

....

....

....

....

....

....

....

....

....

God's Thoughts

Your thoughts—how rare, how beautiful! God, I'll never
comprehend them! I couldn't even begin to count them—
any more than I could count the sand of the sea.
Oh, let me rise in the morning and live always with you!

PSALM 139:17–18 MSG

"For my thoughts are not your thoughts,
neither are your ways my ways,"
declares the LORD.
"As the heavens are higher than the earth,
so are my ways higher than your ways
and my thoughts than your thoughts."

ISAIAH 55:8–9 NIV

Many, O LORD my God,
are the wonders which You have done,
And Your thoughts toward us;
There is none to compare with You.
If I would declare and speak of them,
They would be too numerous to count.

PSALM 40:5 NASB

How great are your works, LORD,
how profound your thoughts!

PSALM 92:5 NIV

The soul is a temple, and God is silently building it by night and by day.
Precious thoughts are building it; unselfish love is building it; all-penetrating faith is building it.

HENRY WARD BEECHER

....

....

....

....

....

....

....

....

....

....

....

....

....

....

....

....

....

....

....

....

....

His Presence

And I have felt
A presence that disturbs me with the joy
Of elevated thoughts; a sense sublime
Of something far more deeply interfused,
Whose dwelling is the light of setting suns.

WILLIAM WORDSWORTH

Know by the light of faith that God is present,
and be content with directing all your actions toward Him.

BROTHER LAWRENCE

God wants us to be present where we are. He invites us to see
and to hear what is around us and, through it all,
to discern the footprints of the Holy.

RICHARD J. FOSTER

I have been away and come back again
many times to this place. Each time I approach,
I regret ever having left. There is a peace here, a serenity,
even before I enter. Just the idea of returning becomes
a balm for the wounds I've collected elsewhere.
Before I can finish even one knock, the door opens wide
and I am in His presence.

BARBARA FARMER

*If I rise on the wings of the dawn, if I settle on the far side of the sea,
even there your hand will guide me, your right hand will hold me fast.*

PSALM 139:9–10 NIV

Seek First

Look at the birds of the air, that they do not sow,
nor reap nor gather into barns, and yet
your heavenly Father feeds them. Are you not worth
much more than they? And who of you by being worried
can add a single hour to his life?

And why are you worried about clothing?
Observe how the lilies of the field grow; they do not toil
nor do they spin, yet I say to you that not even Solomon
in all his glory clothed himself like one of these.
But if God so clothes the grass of the field,
which is alive today and tomorrow is thrown
into the furnace, will He not much more clothe you?
You of little faith!

Do not worry then, saying, "What will we eat?" or
"What will we drink?" or "What will we wear for clothing?"
For...your heavenly Father knows that you
need all these things. But seek first His kingdom
and His righteousness, and all these things
will be added to you.

MATTHEW 6:26–33 ·NASB

Trust the past to the mercy of God,
the present to His love, and the future to His Providence.

AUGUSTINE

....

....

....

....

....

....

....

....

....

....

....

....

....

God With Us

God gets down on His knees among us; gets on our level
and shares Himself with us. He does not reside afar off
and send diplomatic messages, He kneels among us....
God shares Himself generously and graciously.

EUGENE PETERSON

The God who hears is also the one who speaks.
He has spoken and is still speaking. Humanity
remains His project, not its own, and His initiatives
are always at work among us. He certainly
"gives us space," as we say, and this is essential.
But He continues to speak in ways
that serious inquirers can hear if they will.

DALLAS WILLARD

We are always in the presence of God.... There is never
a non-sacred moment! His presence never diminishes.
Our awareness of His presence may falter,
but the reality of His presence never changes.

MAX LUCADO

We are never more fulfilled than when our longing
for God is met by His presence in our lives.

BILLY GRAHAM

My Presence will go with you, and I will give you rest.

EXODUS 33:14 NIV

An Inner Place

Retire from the world each day to some private spot....
Stay in the secret place till the surrounding noises
begin to fade out of your heart and a sense of God's presence
envelops you.... Listen for the inward Voice till you learn to
recognize it.... Give yourself to God and then be what and who
you are without regard to what others think....
Learn to pray inwardly every moment.

A.W. TOZER

Within each of us there is an inner place where
the living God Himself longs to dwell,
our sacred center of belief.

Enter into the inner chamber of your mind. Shut out all things
save God and whatever may aid you in seeking God;
and having barred the door of your chamber, seek Him.

ANSELM OF CANTERBURY

I will remember that when I give Him my heart,
God chooses to live within me—body and soul.
And I know He really is as close as breathing,
His very Spirit inside of me.

*I pray that out of his glorious riches he may strengthen you
with power through his Spirit in your inner being.*

EPHESIANS 3:16 NIV

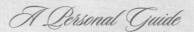

A Personal Guide

But I'll take the hand of those who don't
know the way, who can't see where they're going.
I'll be a personal guide to them, directing them
through unknown country. I'll be right there
to show them what roads to take, make sure they
don't fall into the ditch.
These are the things I'll be doing for them—
sticking with them, not leaving them for a minute.

ISAIAH 42:16 MSG

We can make our plans, but the LORD determines our steps.

PROVERBS 16:9 NLT

For you are my hiding place;
you protect me from trouble.
You surround me with songs of victory.
The LORD says, "I will guide you along
the best pathway for your life.
I will advise you and watch over you."

PSALM 32:7–8 NLT

Whether you turn to the right or to the left,
your ears will hear a voice behind you, saying,
"This is the way; walk in it."

ISAIAH 30:21 NIV

*Heaven often seems distant and unknown, but if He who
made the road...is our guide, we need not fear to lose the way.*

HENRY VAN DYKE

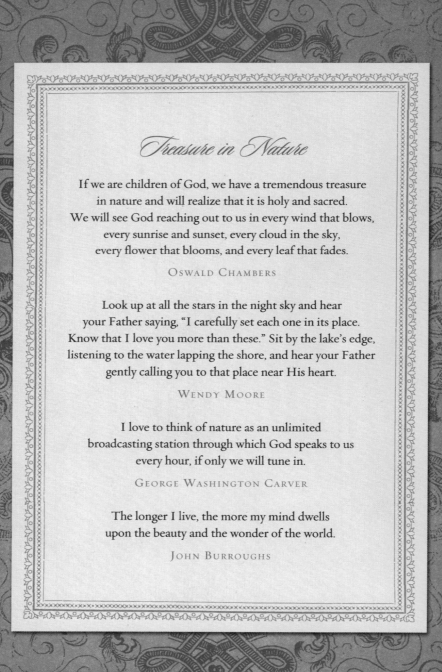

Treasure in Nature

If we are children of God, we have a tremendous treasure
in nature and will realize that it is holy and sacred.
We will see God reaching out to us in every wind that blows,
every sunrise and sunset, every cloud in the sky,
every flower that blooms, and every leaf that fades.

OSWALD CHAMBERS

Look up at all the stars in the night sky and hear
your Father saying, "I carefully set each one in its place.
Know that I love you more than these." Sit by the lake's edge,
listening to the water lapping the shore, and hear your Father
gently calling you to that place near His heart.

WENDY MOORE

I love to think of nature as an unlimited
broadcasting station through which God speaks to us
every hour, if only we will tune in.

GEORGE WASHINGTON CARVER

The longer I live, the more my mind dwells
upon the beauty and the wonder of the world.

JOHN BURROUGHS

The heavens are telling the glory of God;
and the firmament proclaims his handiwork.

PSALM 19:1 NRSV

....

....

....

....

....

....

....

....

....

....

....

....

....

....

Don't Be Afraid

Don't be afraid, I've redeemed you.
I've called your name. You're mine.
When you're in over your head, I'll be there with you.
When you're in rough waters, you will not go down.
When you're between a rock and a hard place, it won't be
a dead end—Because I am GOD, your personal God,
The Holy of Israel, your Savior. I paid a huge price for you...!
That's how much you mean to me!
That's how much I love you!

ISAIAH 43:1–4 MSG

Those who live in the shelter of the Most High
will find rest in the shadow of the Almighty....
Do not be afraid of the terrors of the night,
nor the arrow that flies in the day.
Do not dread the disease that stalks in darkness,
nor the disaster that strikes at midday....
For he will order his angels
to protect you wherever you go.

PSALM 91:1, 5–6, 11 NLT

If God be for us, who can be against us?

ROMANS 8:31 KJV

Do not be afraid to enter the cloud that is settling down on your life.
God is in it. The other side is radiant with His glory.

L. B. COWMAN

....

....

....

....

....

....

....

....

....

....

....

....

....

....

Praise Him

When morning gilds the skies,
My heart awaking cries:
May Jesus Christ be praised!

JOSEPH BARNBY

Does not all nature around me praise God? If I were silent,
I should be an exception to the universe. Does not the
thunder praise Him as it rolls like drums in the march of
the God of armies? Do not the mountains praise Him
when the woods upon their summits wave in adoration?
Does not the lightning write His name in letters of fire?
Has not the whole earth a voice? And shall I, can I, silent be?

CHARLES H. SPURGEON

O God, great and wonderful, who has created the heavens,
dwelling in the light and beauty of it...
teach me to praise You, even as the lark
which offers her song at daybreak.

ISIDORE OF SEVILLE

God specializes in things fresh and firsthand.
His plans for you this year may outshine those of the past....
He's preparing to fill your days
with reasons to give Him praise.

JONI EARECKSON TADA

It is good to praise the LORD and make music to your name, O Most High,
proclaiming your love in the morning and your faithfulness at night.

PSALM 92:1–2 NIV

Have Mercy

Ho, everyone who thirsts, come to the waters;
and you that have no money, come, buy and eat! Come,
buy wine and milk without money and without price.
Why do you spend your money for that which is not bread,
and your labor for that which does not satisfy?
Listen carefully to me, and eat what is good,
and delight yourselves in rich food. Incline your ear,
and come to me; listen, so that you may live. I will make
with you an everlasting covenant.... Seek the LORD while he may
be found, call upon him while he is near;
let the wicked forsake their way, and the unrighteous
their thoughts; let them return to the LORD, that he may
have mercy on them, and to our God,
for he will abundantly pardon.

ISAIAH 55:1–3, 6–7 NRSV

Search me, O God, and know my heart;
test me and know my anxious thoughts.
See if there is any offensive way in me,
and lead me in the way everlasting.

PSALM 139:23–24 NIV

We need more than a watchmaker who winds up the universe and lets it tick.
We need love and mercy and forgiveness and grace—qualities only a personal God can offer.

PHILIP YANCEY

Settled in Solitude

Solitude liberates us from entanglements by carving out a space
from which we can see ourselves and our situation
before the Audience of One. Solitude provides the
private place where we can take our bearings
and so make God our North Star.

Os Guinness

Solitude begins with a time and place for God, and God alone.
If we really believe not only that God exists but also
that He is actively present in our lives—healing, teaching,
guiding—we need to set aside a time and space
to give Him our undivided attention.

Henri J. M. Nouwen

Settle yourself in solitude
and you will come upon Him in yourself.

Teresa of Avila

We must drink deeply from the very Source
the deep calm and peace of interior quietude and refreshment
of God, allowing the pure water of divine grace
to flow plentifully and unceasingly from the Source itself.

Mother Teresa

Let all that I am wait quietly before God, for my hope is in him.

PSALM 62:5 NLT

Showers of Blessings

Bless the LORD, O my soul,
And forget not all His benefits:
Who forgives all your iniquities,
Who heals all your diseases,
Who redeems your life from destruction,
Who crowns you with lovingkindness and tender mercies;
Who satisfies your mouth with good things,
So that your youth is renewed like the eagle's.

PSALM 103:2–5 NKJV

How abundant are the good things that you have stored up
for those who fear you, that you bestow in the sight of all,
on those who take refuge in you.

PSALM 31:19 NIV

The LORD bless you, and keep you;
The LORD make His face shine on you,
And be gracious to you;
The LORD lift up His countenance on you,
And give you peace.

NUMBERS 6:24–26 NASB

I will send down showers in season;
there will be showers of blessing.

EZEKIEL 34:26 NIV

God, who is love—who is, if I may say it this way, made out of love—
simply cannot help but shed blessing on blessing upon us.

HANNAH WHITALL SMITH

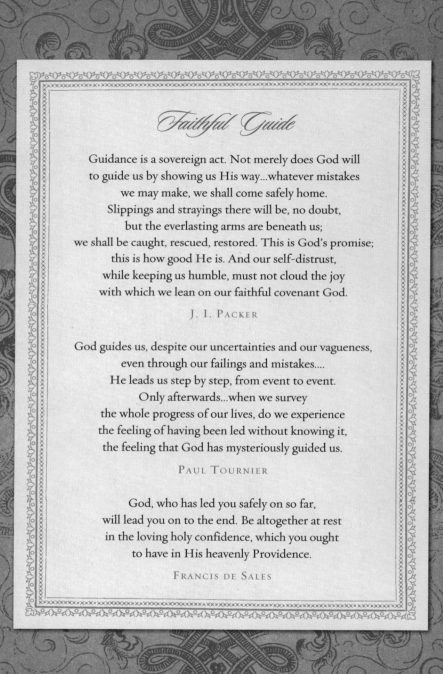

Faithful Guide

Guidance is a sovereign act. Not merely does God will
to guide us by showing us His way...whatever mistakes
we may make, we shall come safely home.
Slippings and strayings there will be, no doubt,
but the everlasting arms are beneath us;
we shall be caught, rescued, restored. This is God's promise;
this is how good He is. And our self-distrust,
while keeping us humble, must not cloud the joy
with which we lean on our faithful covenant God.

J. I. PACKER

God guides us, despite our uncertainties and our vagueness,
even through our failings and mistakes....
He leads us step by step, from event to event.
Only afterwards...when we survey
the whole progress of our lives, do we experience
the feeling of having been led without knowing it,
the feeling that God has mysteriously guided us.

PAUL TOURNIER

God, who has led you safely on so far,
will lead you on to the end. Be altogether at rest
in the loving holy confidence, which you ought
to have in His heavenly Providence.

FRANCIS DE SALES

When we obey him, every path he guides us on
is fragrant with his lovingkindness and his truth.

PSALM 25:10 TLB

....

....

....

....

....

....

....

....

....

....

....

....

....

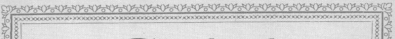

From Sea to Sea

The earth is the LORD's, and the fulness thereof;
the world, and they that dwell therein.
For he hath founded it upon the seas,
and established it upon the floods.

PSALM 24:1–2 KJV

The voice of the LORD is over the waters;
the God of glory thunders,
the LORD thunders over the mighty waters.

PSALM 29:3 NIV

The LORD is the great God,
the great King above all gods.
In his hand are the depths of the earth,
and the mountain peaks belong to him.
The sea is his, for he made it,
and his hands formed the dry land.

PSALM 95:3–5 NIV

Every island of the sea will broadcast
God's fame, the fame of the God of Israel.

ISAIAH 24:15 MSG

He shall have dominion...from sea to sea.

PSALM 72:8 NKJV

Angels bright, heavens high, waters deep, give God the praise.

CHRISTOPHER COLLINS

....

....

....

....

....

....

....

....

....

....

....

....

....

....

Encountering God

God is with us in the midst of our daily, routine lives.
In the middle of cleaning the house or driving
somewhere in the pickup.... Often it's in the middle of the most
mundane task that He lets us know He is there with us.
We realize, then, that there can be no "ordinary" moments
for people who live their lives with Jesus.

MICHAEL CARD

Much of what is sacred is hidden in the ordinary,
everyday moments of our lives. To see something
of the sacred in those moments takes slowing down
so we can live our lives more reflectively.

KEN GIRE

It is not objective proof of God's existence that we want
but the experience of God's presence. That is the miracle
we are really after, and that is also, I think,
the miracle that we really get.

FREDERICK BUECHNER

We encounter God in the ordinariness of life,
not in the search for spiritual highs and extraordinary,
mystical experiences, but in our simple presence in life.

BRENNAN MANNING

God himself shall be with them, and be their God.

REVELATION 21:3 KJV

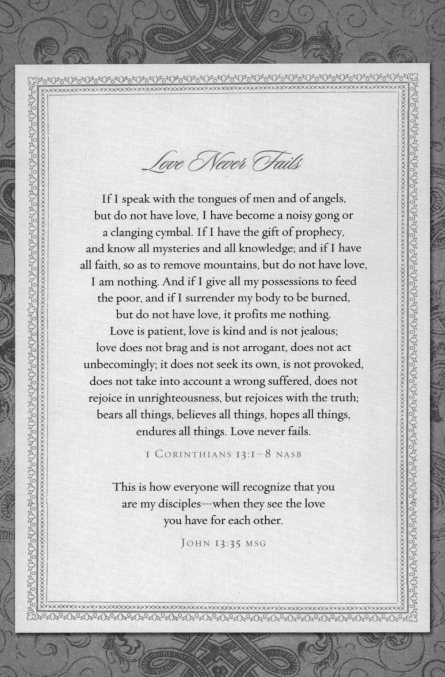

Love Never Fails

If I speak with the tongues of men and of angels,
but do not have love, I have become a noisy gong or
a clanging cymbal. If I have the gift of prophecy,
and know all mysteries and all knowledge; and if I have
all faith, so as to remove mountains, but do not have love,
I am nothing. And if I give all my possessions to feed
the poor, and if I surrender my body to be burned,
but do not have love, it profits me nothing.
Love is patient, love is kind and is not jealous;
love does not brag and is not arrogant, does not act
unbecomingly; it does not seek its own, is not provoked,
does not take into account a wrong suffered, does not
rejoice in unrighteousness, but rejoices with the truth;
bears all things, believes all things, hopes all things,
endures all things. Love never fails.

1 Corinthians 13:1–8 nasb

This is how everyone will recognize that you
are my disciples—when they see the love
you have for each other.

John 13:35 msg

An instant of pure love is more precious to God...
than all other good works together.

JOHN OF THE CROSS

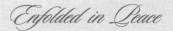

Enfolded in Peace

I will let God's peace infuse every part of today.
As the chaos swirls and life's demands pull at me on all sides,
I will breathe in God's peace that surpasses all understanding.
He has promised that He would set within me
a peace too deeply planted to be affected
by unexpected or exhausting demands.

Life from the Center is a life of unhurried peace and power.
It is simple. It is serene.... We need not get frantic.
He is at the helm. And when our little day is done,
we lie down quietly in peace, for all is well.

THOMAS R. KELLY

Calm me, O Lord, as you stilled the storm,
Still me, O Lord, keep me from harm.
Let all the tumult within me cease,
Enfold me, Lord, in your peace.

CELTIC TRADITIONAL

God cannot give us a happiness and peace apart from Himself,
because it is not there. There is no such thing.

C. S. LEWIS

God's peace...is far more wonderful than the human mind can understand.
His peace will keep your thoughts and your hearts quiet and at rest.

PHILIPPIANS 4:7 TLB

His Imprint

The God of the universe—the One who created everything
and holds it all in His hand—created each of us in His image,
to bear His likeness, His imprint. It is only when Christ
dwells within our hearts, radiating the pure light of His love
through our humanity, that we discover who we are
and what we were intended to be. There is no other joy
that reaches as deep or as wide or as high—
there is no other joy that is more complete.

WENDY MOORE

In the very beginning it was God who formed us by His Word.
He made us in His own image. God was spirit and He
gave us a spirit so that He could come into us
and mingle His own life with our life.

MADAME JEANNE GUYON

Made in His image, we can have real meaning,
and we can have real knowledge through
what He has communicated to us.

FRANCIS SCHAEFFER

Every single act of love bears the imprint of God.

For in Him all the fullness of Deity dwells in bodily form,
and in Him you have been made complete.

COLOSSIANS 2:9–10 NASB

....

....

....

....

....

....

....

....

....

....

....

....

....

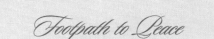

Footpath to Peace

To be glad of life, because it gives you the chance to love
and to work and to play and to look up at the stars;
to be satisfied with your possessions, but not contented
with yourself until you have made the best of them...
to think seldom of your enemies, often of your friends,
and every day of Christ; and to spend as much time as you can,
with body and with spirit in God's out-of-doors—
these are little guideposts on the footpath to peace.

HENRY VAN DYKE

The thought of You stirs us so deeply that we
cannot be content unless we praise You,
because You have made us for yourself
and our hearts find no peace until they rest in You.

AUGUSTINE

The heart is rich when it is content, and it is always content
when its desires are fixed on God. Nothing can bring
greater happiness than doing God's will for the love of God.

MIGUEL FEBRES CORDERO MUÑOZ

God's peace is joy resting. His joy is peace dancing.

F. F. BRUCE

The LORD will give strength unto his people;
the LORD will bless his people with peace.

PSALM 29:11 KJV

The Word of God

For the word of God is alive and active.
Sharper than any double-edged sword, it penetrates
even to dividing soul and spirit, joints and marrow;
it judges the thoughts and attitudes of the heart.
Nothing in all creation is hidden from God's sight.
Everything is uncovered and laid bare before
the eyes of him to whom we must give account.

HEBREWS 4:12–13 NIV

The rain and snow come down from the heavens
and stay on the ground to water the earth.
They cause the grain to grow, producing seed
for the farmer and bread for the hungry.
It is the same with my word.
I send it out, and it always produces fruit.
It will accomplish all I want it to,
and it will prosper everywhere I send it....
Where once there were thorns, cypress trees will grow.
Where nettles grew, myrtles will sprout up.
These events will bring great honor to the LORD's name;
they will be an everlasting sign of his power and love.

ISAIAH 55:10–11, 13 NLT

Not one word has failed of all His good promise.

1 KINGS 8:56 NASB

God is the God of promise. He keeps His word,
even when that seems impossible.

COLIN URQUHART

....

....

....

....

....

....

....

....

....

....

....

....

....

....

In God's Thoughts

Tonight I will sleep beneath Your feet, O Lord
of the mountains and valleys, ruler of the trees and vines.
I will rest in Your love, with You protecting me as a father
protects his children, with You watching over me
as a mother watches over her children. Then tomorrow
the sun will rise and I may not know where I am;
but I know that You will guide my footsteps.

We have been in God's thought from all eternity,
and in His creative love, His attention never leaves us.

MICHAEL QUOIST

Life in the presence of God
should be known to us in conscious experience.
It is a life to be enjoyed every moment of every day.

A. W. TOZER

Have confidence in God's mercy, for when you think
He is a long way from you, He is often quite near.

THOMAS À KEMPIS

When I walk by the wayside, He is along with me....
Amid all my forgetfulness of Him, He never forgets me.

THOMAS CHALMERS

The LORD searches all hearts, and understands every intent of the thoughts.
If you seek Him, He will let you find Him.

1 CHRONICLES 28:9 NASB

The Stillness

And he said, Go forth, and stand upon the mount before
the LORD. And, behold, the LORD passed by, and a great
and strong wind rent the mountains...but the LORD
was not in the wind: and after the wind an earthquake;
but the LORD was not in the earthquake: And after the
earthquake a fire; but the LORD was not in the fire:
and after the fire a still small voice. And it was so.

1 KINGS 19:11–13 KJV

Then they cried out to the LORD in their trouble,
and he brought them out of their distress.
He stilled the storm to a whisper;
the waves of the sea were hushed.
They were glad when it grew calm,
and he guided them to their desired haven.

PSALM 107:28–30 NIV

The LORD's justice will dwell in the desert,
his righteousness live in the fertile field.
The fruit of that righteousness will be peace;
its effect will be quietness and confidence forever.

ISAIAH 32:16-17 NIV

For you are God, my only safe haven.

PSALM 43:2 NLT

Nothing in all creation is so like God as stillness.

MEISTER ECKHART

....

....

....

....

....

....

....

....

....

....

....

....

....

....

....

God Is Here!

What we need to know, of course, is not just
that God exists, not just that beyond the steely brightness
of the stars there is a cosmic intelligence...
but that there is a God right here in the thick of
our day-by-day lives who may not be writing messages
about Himself in the stars but in one way or another
is trying to get messages through our blindness.

FREDERICK BUECHNER

God is here! I hear His voice
While thrushes make the woods rejoice.
I touch His robe each time I place
My hand against a pansy's face.
I breathe His breath if I but pass
Verbenas trailing through the grass.
God is here! From every tree
His leafy fingers beckon me.

MADELEINE AARON

God is here. I have joyously discovered that He is always
"up to something" in my life, and I am learning to quit
second-guessing Him and simply trust the process.

GLORIA GAITHER

Let the glory of the LORD endure forever;
let the LORD be glad in His works.

PSALM 104:31 NASB

....

....

....

....

....

....

....

....

....

....

....

....

....

....

My Help

I will lift up mine eyes unto the hills,
from whence cometh my help.
My help cometh from the LORD,
which made heaven and earth.
He will not suffer thy foot to be moved:
he that keepeth thee will not slumber.
Behold, he that keepeth Israel shall neither
slumber nor sleep. The LORD is thy keeper:
the LORD is thy shade upon thy right hand.
The sun shall not smite thee by day,
nor the moon by night. The LORD shall preserve thee
from all evil: he shall preserve thy soul.
The LORD shall preserve thy going out and thy coming
in from this time forth, and even for evermore.

PSALM 121:1–8 KJV

I trust in your unfailing love.
I will rejoice because you have rescued me.
I will sing to the LORD
because he is good to me.

PSALM 13:5–6 NLT

We have a Father in heaven who is almighty, who loves His children as He loves His only-begotten Son, and whose very joy and delight it is to...help them at all times and under all circumstances.

GEORGE MÜELLER

Everyday Prayer

Prayer is such an ordinary, everyday, mundane thing.
Certainly, people who pray are no more saints than the rest of us.
Rather, they are people who want to share a life with God,
to love and be loved, to speak and to listen,
to work and to be at rest in the presence of God.

ROBERTA BONDI

Being able to bow in prayer as the day begins or ends
gives expression to the frustrations and concerns
that might not otherwise be ventilated.
On the other end of that prayer line is a loving heavenly Father
who has promised to hear and answer our petitions.

DR. JAMES DOBSON

Nothing in your daily life is so insignificant
and so inconsequential that God will not
help you by answering your prayer.

OLE HALLESBY

Can we find a friend so faithful,
Who will all our sorrows share?
Jesus knows our every weakness:
Take it to the Lord in prayer.

GEORGE SCRIVEN

Cast thy burden upon the LORD, and he shall sustain thee.

PSALM 55:22 KJV

To All Generations

Blessed be the name of God from age to age,
for wisdom and power are his. He changes times and seasons,
deposes kings and sets up kings; he gives wisdom to the wise
and knowledge to those who have understanding.
He reveals deep and hidden things; he knows what
is in the darkness, and light dwells with him.

DANIEL 2:20–22 NRSV

Know therefore that the LORD your God is God;
he is the faithful God, keeping his covenant of love
to a thousand generations of those who love him
and keep his commands.

DEUTERONOMY 7:9 NIV

I will sing of the mercies of the LORD for ever: with my mouth
will I make known thy faithfulness to all generations.

PSALM 89:1 KJV

For he is the living God
and he endures forever;
his kingdom will not be destroyed,
his dominion will never end.

DANIEL 6:26 NIV

In following our everlasting God,
we touch the things that last forever

....

....

....

....

....

....

....

....

....

....

....

....

....

A Life Transformed

To pray is to change. This is a great grace. How good of God
to provide a path whereby our lives can be taken over by love
and joy and peace and patience and kindness
and goodness and faithfulness and gentleness and self-control.

RICHARD J. FOSTER

For God is, indeed, a wonderful Father who longs
to pour out His mercy upon us, and whose majesty
is so great that He can transform us from deep within.

TERESA OF AVILA

God is always on duty in the temple of your heart, His home....
It is the place where Someone takes your trouble
and changes it into His treasure.

BARBARA JOHNSON

A life transformed by the power of God
is always a marvel and a miracle.

GERALDINE NICHOLAS

Grace is the central invitation to life and the final word.
It's the beckoning nudge and the overwhelming,
undeserved mercy that urges us to change and grow,
and then gives us the power to pull it off.

TIM HANSEL

Create in me a clean heart, O God;
and renew a right spirit within me.

PSALM 51:10 KJV

....

....

....

....

....

....

....

....

....

....

....

....

....

....

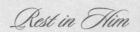

Rest in Him

Truly my soul finds rest in God;
my salvation comes from him.
Truly he is my rock and my salvation;
he is my fortress, I will never be shaken....
My salvation and my honor depend on God;
he is my mighty rock, my refuge.
Trust in him at all times, you people;
pour out your hearts to him,
for God is our refuge....
One thing God has spoken,
two things I have heard:
"Power belongs to you, God,
and with you, Lord, is unfailing love."

PSALM 62:1–2,7–8,11–12 NIV

The fulfillment of God's promise depends entirely
on trusting God and his way, and then simply embracing him
and what he does. God's promise arrives as pure gift.

ROMANS 4:16 MSG

Come away by yourselves to a secluded place and rest a while.

MARK 6:31 NASB

Rest in the LORD, and wait patiently for him.

PSALM 37:7 KJV

God provides resting places as well as working places. Rest, then,
and be thankful when He brings you, wearied, to a wayside well.

L. B. COWMAN

....

....

....

....

....

....

....

....

....

....

....

....

....

....

My Father's World

Wherever we look in the realm of nature, we see evidence
for God's design and exquisite care for His creatures.
Whether we examine the cosmos on its largest scale or its tiniest,
His handiwork is evident.... God's fingerprints are visible.

DR. HUGH ROSS

Above all give me grace to use these beauties
of earth without me and this eager stirring of life within me
as a means whereby my soul may rise from creature to Creator,
and from nature to nature's God.

JOHN BAILLIE

Beauty puts a face on God. When we gaze at nature,
at a loved one, at a work of art, our soul immediately
recognizes and is drawn to the face of God.

MARGARET BROWNLEY

This is my Father's world;
He shines in all that's fair.
In the rustling grass I hear Him pass;
He speaks to me everywhere.

MALTBIE D. BABCOCK

*I am the light of the world. Whoever follows me will
never walk in darkness, but will have the light of life.*

JOHN 8:12 NIV

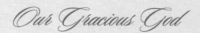

Our Gracious God

The LORD longs to be gracious to you;
therefore he will rise up to show you compassion.
For the LORD is a God of justice.
Blessed are all who wait for him!

ISAIAH 30:18 NIV

Even before he made the world, God loved us and
chose us in Christ to be holy and without fault in his eyes.
God decided in advance to adopt us into his own family
by bringing us to himself through Jesus Christ.
This is what he wanted to do, and it gave him great pleasure.
So we praise God for the glorious grace he has
poured out on us who belong to his dear Son.

EPHESIANS 1:4–6 NLT

God is sheer mercy and grace;
not easily angered, he's rich in love....
As high as the heaven is over the earth,
so strong is his love to those who fear him.

PSALM 103:8, 11 MSG

You, Lord, are a compassionate and gracious God,
slow to anger, abounding in love and faithfulness.

PSALM 86:15 NIV

Lord...give me only Your love and Your grace.
With this I am rich enough, and I have no more to ask.

IGNATIUS OF LOYOLA

A Firsthand Experience

Listening to God is a firsthand experience.... God invites *you*
to vacation in His splendor. He invites *you* to feel
the touch of His hand. He invites *you* to feast at His table.
He wants to spend time with *you*.

MAX LUCADO

Prayer is language used to respond to the most that has
been said to us, with the potential for saying all that is in us.

EUGENE PETERSON

In extravagance of soul we seek His face.
In generosity of heart we glean His gentle touch.
In excessiveness of spirit we love Him,
and His love comes back to us a hundredfold.

TRICIA McCARY RHODES

Prayer is neither chiefly begging for things, nor is it
merely self-communion; it is that loftiest experience
within the reach of any soul, communion with God.

HARRY EMERSON FOSDICK

That is God's call to us—simply to be people who are content
to live close to Him and to renew the kind of life in which
the closeness is felt and experienced.

THOMAS MERTON

God, your God, will cut away the thick calluses on your heart and your children's hearts, freeing you to love God, your God, with your whole heart and soul and live, really live.

DEUTERONOMY 30:6 MSG

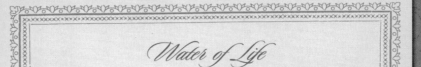

Water of Life

For I will pour water on the thirsty land,
and streams on the dry ground; I will pour out my Spirit
on your offspring, and my blessing on your descendants.

ISAIAH 44:3 NIV

Is anyone thirsty? Come!
All who will, come and drink,
Drink freely of the Water of Life!

REVELATION 22:17 MSG

Let the redeemed of the LORD say so....
They were hungry and thirsty;
Their soul fainted within them.
Then they cried out to the LORD in their trouble;
He delivered them out of their distresses....
Let them give thanks to the LORD for His lovingkindness...
For He has satisfied the thirsty soul,
And the hungry soul He has filled with what is good.

PSALM 107:2, 5–6, 8–9 NASB

Jesus [said], "Anyone who is thirsty may come to me!
Anyone who believes in me may come and drink!
For the Scriptures declare, 'Rivers of living water
will flow from his heart.'"

JOHN 7:37–38 NLT

Jesus...has been waiting all along for us to bring
our needy selves to Him and receive from Him that eternal water.

DORIS GAILEY

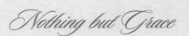

Nothing but Grace

Grace is no stationary thing, it is ever becoming.
It is flowing straight out of God's heart.
Grace does nothing but re-form and convey God.
Grace makes the soul conformable to the will of God.
God, the ground of the soul, and grace go together.

MEISTER ECKHART

If heaven were by merit, it would never be heaven to me,
for if I were in it I should say, "I am sure I am here by mistake;
I am sure this is not my place; I have no claim to it."
But if it be of grace and not of works,
then we may walk into heaven with boldness.

CHARLES H. SPURGEON

Grace and gratitude belong together like heaven and earth.
Grace evokes gratitude like the voice an echo.
Gratitude follows grace as thunder follows lightning.

KARL BARTH

There is nothing but God's grace.
We walk upon it; we breathe it; we live and die by it;
it makes the nails and axles of the universe.

ROBERT LOUIS STEVENSON

For your kingdom is an everlasting kingdom. You rule throughout all generations.
The LORD always keeps his promises; he is gracious in all he does.

PSALM 145:13 NLT

The Lord's Prayer

Our Father which art in heaven, Hallowed be thy name.
Thy kingdom come. Thy will be done in earth, as it is in heaven.
Give us this day our daily bread. And forgive us our debts,
as we forgive our debtors. And lead us not into temptation,
but deliver us from evil: For thine is the kingdom,
and the power, and the glory, for ever. Amen.

MATTHEW 6:9–13 KJV

As the deer pants for streams of water,
so my soul pants for you, my God.
My soul thirsts for God, for the living God.

PSALM 42:1–2 NIV

Embrace this God-life. Really embrace it,
and nothing will be too much for you.... That's why
I urge you to pray for absolutely everything,
ranging from small to large. Include everything
as you embrace this God-life,
and you'll get God's everything.

MARK 11:22, 24 MSG

By day the LORD directs his love,
at night his song is with me—
a prayer to the God of my life.

PSALM 42:8 NIV

They who seek the throne of grace find that throne in every place;
If we live a life of prayer, God is present everywhere.

OLIVER HOLDEN

All Is Well

A living, loving God can and does make His presence felt,
can and does speak to us in the silence of our hearts,
can and does warm and caress us till we no longer
doubt that He is near, that He is here.

BRENNAN MANNING

Today Jesus is working just as wonderful works as
when He created the heaven and the earth. His wondrous grace,
His wonderful omnipotence, is for His child who needs Him
and who trusts Him, even today.

CHARLES HURLBURT AND T. C. HORTON

Friendships, family ties, the companionship of little children,
an autumn forest flung in prodigality against a deep blue sky,
the intricate design and haunting fragrance of a flower,
the counterpoint of a Bach fugue or the melodic line
of a Beethoven sonata, the fluted note of bird song,
the glowing glory of a sunset: the world is
aflame with things of eternal moment.

E. MARGARET CLARKSON

Before me, even as behind,
God is, and all is well.

JOHN GREENLEAF WHITTIER

From everlasting to everlasting, thou art God.

PSALM 90:2 KJV

....

....

....

....

....

....

....

....

....

....

....

....

....

....

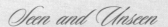

Seen and Unseen

They know the truth about God because he has
made it obvious to them. For ever since the world was created,
people have seen the earth and sky.
Through everything God made, they can
clearly see his invisible qualities—his eternal power
and divine nature. So they have
no excuse for not knowing God.

ROMANS 1:19–20 NLT

Now faith is confidence in what we hope for and
assurance about what we do not see.... By faith we
understand that the universe was formed at God's
command, so that what is seen was not made out of
what was visible.... And without faith it is impossible
to please God, because anyone who comes
to him must believe that he exists and that he
rewards those who earnestly seek him.

HEBREWS 11:1, 3, 6 NIV

So we fix our eyes not on what is seen, but on what is unseen,
since what is seen is temporary, but what is unseen is eternal.

2 CORINTHIANS 4:18 NIV

*You...live in time and eternity simultaneously,
and eternity makes time significant.*

E. STANLEY JONES

....

....

....

....

....

....

....

....

....

....

....

....

....

Overflowing Praise

All enjoyment spontaneously overflows into praise....
The world rings with praise...walkers praising the countryside,
players praising their favorite game.... I think we delight to praise
what we enjoy because the praise not merely expresses but
completes the enjoyment; it is the appointed consummation.

C. S. LEWIS

God's pursuit of praise from us and our pursuit
of pleasure in Him are one and the same pursuit.
God's quest to be glorified and our quest to be satisfied
reach their goal in this one experience:
our delight in God, which overflows in praise.

JOHN PIPER

Like supernatural effervescence, praise will
sometimes bubble up from the joy of simply knowing Christ.
Praise like that is...delight. Pure pleasure! But praise
can also be supernatural determination. A decisive action.
Praise like that is...quiet resolve.
Fixed devotion. Strength of spirit.

JONI EARECKSON TADA

Earth, with her thousand voices, praises God.

SAMUEL TAYLOR COLERIDGE

O sing unto the LORD a new song:
sing unto the LORD, all the earth.

PSALM 96:1 KJV

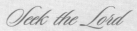

Seek the Lord

The God who made the world and everything in it
is the Lord of heaven and earth.... He himself gives
everyone life and breath and everything else....
God did this so that they would seek him
and perhaps reach out for him and find him,
though he is not far from any one of us. "For in him we live,
and move, and have our being."

ACTS 17:24–25, 27–28 NIV

I'm asking GOD for one thing,
only one thing:
To live with him in his house
my whole life long.
I'll contemplate his beauty;
I'll study at his feet.

PSALM 27:4 MSG

Keep on asking, and you will receive what you ask for.
Keep on seeking, and you will find. Keep on knocking,
and the door will be opened to you.

MATTHEW 7:7 NLT

I love those who love me; and those who
diligently seek me will find me.

PROVERBS 8:17 NASB

God is not an elusive dream or a phantom to chase,
but a divine person to know. He does not avoid us,
but seeks us. When we seek Him, the contact is instantaneous.

NEVA COYLE

....

....

....

....

....

....

....

....

....

....

....

....

....

God Listens

You can talk to God because God listens.
Your voice matters in heaven. He takes you very seriously.
When you enter His presence, the attendants turn to you
to hear your voice. No need to fear that you will be ignored.
Even if you stammer or stumble, even if what you have to say
impresses no one, it impresses God—and He listens.

MAX LUCADO

When we call on God, He bends down His ear to listen,
as a father bends down to listen to his little child.

ELIZABETH CHARLES

Jesus is always waiting for us in silence. In that silence,
He will listen to us; there He will speak to our soul,
and there we will hear His voice.

MOTHER TERESA

Prayer is meant to be a part of our lives, like breathing,
thinking, and talking. Isn't that great? God is portable.

GLORIA GAITHER

God listens in compassion and love,
just like we do when our children come to us.
He delights in our presence.

RICHARD J. FOSTER

I love the LORD because he hears my voice and my prayer for mercy.
Because he bends down and listens, I will pray as long as I have breath!

PSALM 116:1–2 NLT

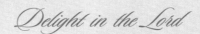

Delight in the Lord

Delight yourself in the LORD,
And He shall give you the desires of your heart.
Commit your way to the LORD;
Trust also in Him, and He shall bring it to pass.
He shall bring forth your righteousness as the light,
And your justice as the noonday.

PSALM 37:4–6 NKJV

Send me your light and your faithful care,
let them lead me;
let them bring me to your holy mountain,
to the place where you dwell.
Then will I go to the altar of God,
to God, my joy and my delight.

PSALM 43:3–4 NIV

I am overwhelmed with joy in the LORD my God!
For he has dressed me with the clothing of salvation
and draped me in a robe of righteousness.
I am like a bridegroom in his wedding suit
or a bride with her jewels.

ISAIAH 61:10 NLT

Let all who seek You rejoice and be glad in You.

PSALM 40:16 NASB

Our fulfillment comes in knowing God's glory,
loving Him for it, and delighting in it.

....

....

....

....

....

....

....

....

....

....

....

....

....

....

New Light

Open wide the windows of our spirits and fill us full of light;
open wide the door of our hearts, that we may receive
and entertain Thee with all our powers of adoration.

CHRISTINA ROSSETTI

I cannot open mine eyes,
But Thou art ready there to catch
My morning soul, and sacrifice....
Teach me Thy love to know;
That this new light, which now I see,
May both the work and Workman show:
Then by a sunbeam I will climb to Thee.

GEORGE HERBERT

We are His only witnesses. God is counting on each of us.
No angel has been given the job. We are the lanterns—
Christ is the light inside.

OLETA SPRAY

Nothing can compare to the beauty
and greatness of the soul in which our King
dwells in His full majesty. No earthly fire can
compare with the light of its blazing love.

TERESA OF AVILA

The LORD is my light and my salvation—whom shall I fear?
The LORD is the stronghold of my life—of whom shall I be afraid?

PSALM 27:1 NIV

Boundless Strength

I ask—ask the God of our Master, Jesus Christ,
the God of glory—to make you intelligent and discerning
in knowing him personally, your eyes focused and clear,
so that you can see exactly what it is he is calling you to do,
grasp the immensity of this glorious way of life he has
for his followers, oh, the utter extravagance of his work in us
who trust him—endless energy, boundless strength!

EPHESIANS 1:17–19 MSG

The LORD is great, and greatly to be praised....
The LORD made the heavens. Honour and majesty are
before him: strength and beauty are in his sanctuary....
Give unto the LORD glory and strength.
Give unto the LORD the glory due unto his name.

PSALM 96:4–8 KJV

The LORD is my rock and my fortress and my deliverer,
My God, my rock, in whom I take refuge;
My shield and the horn of my salvation, my stronghold.
I call upon the LORD, who is worthy to be praised.

PSALM 18:2–3 NASB

I can do all things through Christ who strengthens me.

PHILIPPIANS 4:13 NKJV

Strength, rest, guidance, grace, help, sympathy, love—
all from God to us! What a list of blessings!

EVELYN STENBOCK

Totally Aware

God is every moment totally aware of each one of us.
Totally aware in intense concentration and love....
No one passes through any area of life, happy or tragic,
without the attention of God with him.

EUGENIA PRICE

Because God is responsible for our welfare,
we are told to cast all our care upon Him, for He cares for us.
God says, "I'll take the burden—don't give it a thought—
leave it to Me." God is keenly aware that we
are dependent upon Him for life's necessities.

BILLY GRAHAM

God not only knows us, but He values us highly
in spite of all He knows.... You and I are the creatures
He prizes above the rest of His creation.
We are made in His image, and He sacrificed His Son
that each one of us might be one with Him.

JOHN FISHER

God knows everything about us. And He cares about everything.
Moreover, He can manage every situation. And He loves us!
Surely this is enough to open the wellsprings of joy.

HANNAH WHITALL SMITH

Live carefree before God; he is most careful with you.

1 PETER 5:7 MSG

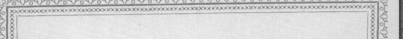

Think on These Things

Whatsoever things are true, whatsoever things are honest,
whatsoever things are just, whatsoever things are pure,
whatsoever things are lovely, whatsoever things are of
good report; if there be any virtue, and if there be
any praise, think on these things.

PHILIPPIANS 4:8 KJV

Let us hold unswervingly to the hope we profess,
for he who promised is faithful. And let us consider
how we may spur one another on toward love and good deeds,
not giving up meeting together, as some are in the habit of doing,
but encouraging one another—
and all the more as you see the Day approaching.

HEBREWS 10:23–25 NIV

The wisdom from above is first of all pure.
It is also peace loving, gentle at all times, and willing
to yield to others. It is full of mercy and good deeds.
It shows no favoritism and is always sincere.
And those who are peacemakers will plant seeds of peace
and reap a harvest of righteousness.

JAMES 3:17–18 NLT

Only to sit and think of God, oh what a joy it is! To think the thought,
to breathe the Name: Earth has no higher bliss.

FREDERICK W. FABER

....

....

....

....

....

....

....

....

....

....

....

....

....

....

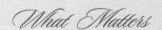

What Matters

The God who created, names, and numbers
the stars in the heavens also numbers the hairs of my head....
He pays attention to very big things and to very small ones.
What matters to me matters to Him,
and that changes my life.

ELISABETH ELLIOT

What matters supremely is not the fact that I know God,
but the larger fact which underlies it—
the fact that *He knows me*. I am graven on the palms of His hands.
I am never out of His mind. All my knowledge of Him
depends on His sustained initiative in knowing me.
I know Him because He first knew me,
and continues to know me.

J. I. PACKER

One hundred years from today your present income
will be inconsequential. One hundred years from now
it won't matter if you got that big break....
It will greatly matter that you knew God.

DAVID SHIBLEY

What really matters is what happens in us, not to us.

D. JAMES KENNEDY

I consider all things to be loss in view of the surpassing
value of knowing Christ Jesus my Lord.

PHILIPPIANS 3:8 NASB

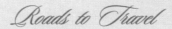

Roads to Travel

GOD, teach me lessons for living so I can stay the course.
Give me insight so I can do what you tell me—my whole life
one long, obedient response. Guide me down the road
of your commandments; I love traveling this freeway!
Give me a bent for your words of wisdom,
and not for piling up loot.
Divert my eyes from toys and trinkets,
invigorate me on the pilgrim way.

PSALM 119:33–37 MSG

Enter through the narrow gate. For wide is the gate
and broad is the road that leads to destruction,
and many enter through it. But small is the gate and narrow
the road that leads to life, and only a few find it.

MATTHEW 7:13–14 NIV

How blessed all those in whom you live,
whose lives become roads you travel; they wind
through lonesome valleys, come upon brooks,
discover cool springs and pools brimming with rain!
God-traveled, these roads curve up the mountain,
and at the last turn—Zion! God in full view!

PSALM 84:5–7 MSG

Joy is really a road sign pointing us to God.
Once we have found God...we no longer
need to trouble ourselves so much about the quest for joy.

C. S. LEWIS

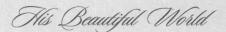

His Beautiful World

Forbid that I should walk through Thy beautiful world
with unseeing eyes: Forbid that the lure of the market-place
should ever entirely steal my heart away from the love
of the open acres and the green trees:
Forbid that under the low roof of workshop or office or study
I should ever forget Thy great overarching sky.

JOHN BAILLIE

Our Creator would never have made such lovely days,
and given us the deep hearts to enjoy them,
above and beyond all thought,
unless we were meant to be immortal.

NATHANIEL HAWTHORNE

When one has once fully entered the realm of love, the world—
no matter how imperfect—becomes rich and beautiful,
for it consists solely of opportunities for love.

SØREN KIERKEGAARD

As a countenance is made beautiful
by the soul's shining through it,
so the world is beautiful by the shining through it of God.

FRIEDRICH HEINRICH JACOBI

The whole earth is full of his glory.

ISAIAH 6:3 KJV

God's Word

With my whole heart have I sought thee:
O let me not wander from thy commandments.
Thy word have I hid in mine heart,
that I might not sin against thee.... I will not forget thy word.

PSALM 119:10–11, 16 KJV

All Scripture is inspired by God and is useful
to teach us what is true and to make us realize what is
wrong in our lives. It corrects us when we are wrong
and teaches us to do what is right.

2 TIMOTHY 3:16 NLT

Not one word of all the good words which the
LORD your God spoke concerning you has failed;
all have been fulfilled for you, not one of them has failed.

JOSHUA 23:14 NASB

Your word, LORD, is eternal;
it stands firm in the heavens.
Your faithfulness continues through all generations;
you established the earth, and it endures.
Your laws endure to this day,
for all things serve you.

PSALM 119:89–91 NIV

*When we give the Word of God space to live in our heart, the Spirit of God
will use it to take root, penetrating the earthiest recesses of our lives.*

KEN GIRE

....

....

....

....

....

....

....

....

....

....

....

....

....

The Beauty of God's Peace

In comparison with this big world, the human heart
is only a small thing. Though the world is so large,
it is utterly unable to satisfy this tiny heart.
Our ever-growing soul and its capacities can be satisfied only
in the infinite God. As water is restless until it reaches its level,
so the soul has no peace until it rests in God.

SADHU SUNDAR SINGH

From the world we see, hear, and touch, we behold
inspired visions that reveal God's glory.
In the sun's light, we catch warm rays of grace and glimpse
His eternal design. In the birds' song, we hear His voice
and it reawakens our desire for Him. At the wind's touch,
we feel His Spirit and sense our eternal existence.

WENDY MOORE

Drop Thy still dews of quietness
till all our strivings cease;
take from our souls the strain and stress,
and let our ordered lives confess
the beauty of Thy peace.

JOHN GREENLEAF WHITTIER

Be still, and know that I am God.

PSALM 46:10 KJV

....

....

....

....

....

....

....

....

....

....

....

....

....

....

A River of Delights

Your love, LORD, reaches to the heavens,
your faithfulness to the skies. Your righteousness is like
the highest mountains, your justice like the great deep....
How priceless is your unfailing love, O God!
People take refuge in the shadow of your wings.
They feast on the abundance of your house;
you give them drink from your river of delights.
For with you is the fountain of life;
in your light we see light.

PSALM 36:5–9 NIV

Jesus answered, "Everyone who drinks this water
will be thirsty again, but whoever drinks
the water I give them will never thirst.
Indeed, the water I give them will become in them
a spring of water welling up to eternal life."

JOHN 4:13–14 NIV

I am the Alpha and the Omega—the Beginning and the End.
To all who are thirsty I will give freely
from the springs of the water of life.

REVELATION 21:6 NLT

*God's love is like a river springing up in the Divine Substance
and flowing endlessly through His creation, filling all things
with life and goodness and strength.*

THOMAS MERTON

Infinite Love

An infinite God can give all of Himself to each of His children.
He does not distribute Himself that each may have a part,
but to each one He gives all of Himself as fully
as if there were no others.... His love has not changed.
It hasn't cooled off, and it needs no increase because
He has already loved us with infinite love
and there is no way that infinitude can be increased....
He is the same yesterday, today, and forever!

A. W. TOZER

Infinite and yet personal, personal and yet infinite,
God may be trusted because He is the True One. He is true,
He acts truly, and He speaks truly.... God's truthfulness
is therefore foundational for His trustworthiness.

OS GUINNESS

At the very heart and foundation of all God's dealings with us,
however dark and mysterious they may be,
we must dare to believe in and assert the infinite,
unmerited, and unchanging love of God.

L. B. COWMAN

Take a long, hard look. See how great he is—infinite,
greater than anything you could ever imagine or figure out!

JOB 36:26 MSG

God Is Our Refuge

Hear my cry, O God; Give heed to my prayer.
From the end of the earth I call to You when my heart is faint;
Lead me to the rock that is higher than I.
For You have been a refuge for me,
A tower of strength against the enemy.
Let me dwell in Your tent forever;
Let me take refuge in the shelter of Your wings.

PSALM 61:1–4 NASB

Every word of God is flawless;
he is a shield to those who take refuge in him.

PROVERBS 30:5 NIV

Whom have I in heaven but You?
And besides You, I desire nothing on earth.
My flesh and my heart may fail,
But God is the strength of my heart and my portion forever....
As for me, the nearness of God is my good;
I have made the Lord GOD my refuge.

PSALM 73:25–26, 28 NASB

When God has become...our refuge and our fortress, then we can reach out to Him
in the midst of a broken world and feel at home while still on the way.

HENRI J. M. NOUWEN

Every Need

God wants nothing from us except our needs,
and these furnish Him with room to display His bounty
when He supplies them freely.... Not what I have,
but what I do not have, is the first point of contact
between my soul and God.

CHARLES H. SPURGEON

Jesus Christ has brought every need, every joy,
every gratitude, every hope of ours before God.
He accompanies us and brings us into the presence of God.

DIETRICH BONHOEFFER

God is waiting for us to come to Him with our needs....
God's throne room is always open.... Every single believer
in the whole world could walk into the throne room
all at one time, and it would not even be crowded.

CHARLES STANLEY

The "air" which our souls need also envelops
all of us at all times and on all sides.
God is round about us...on every hand,
with many-sided and all-sufficient grace.

OLE HALLESBY

My God is changeless in his love for me
and he will come and help me.

PSALM 59:10 TLB

....

....

....

....

....

....

....

....

....

....

....

....

....

....

Celebrate His Goodness

I will exalt you, my God the King;
I will praise your name for ever and ever....
Great is the LORD and most worthy of praise;
his greatness no one can fathom.
One generation will commend your works to another;
they tell of your mighty acts.
They speak of the glorious splendor of your majesty—
and I will meditate on your wonderful works.
They tell of the power of your awesome works—
and I will proclaim your great deeds.
They celebrate your abundant goodness
and joyfully sing of your righteousness.

PSALM 145:1, 3–7 NIV

Praise ye the LORD. Praise God in his sanctuary:
praise him in the firmament of his power.
Praise him for his mighty acts:
praise him according to his excellent greatness.
Praise him with the sound of the trumpet:
praise him with the psaltery and harp. Praise him with
the timbrel and dance.... Let every thing that hath breath
praise the LORD. Praise ye the LORD.

PSALM 150:1–4, 6 KJV

*Life itself, every bit of health that we enjoy, every hour of liberty
and free enjoyment...comes from the hand of God.*

BILLY GRAHAM

....

....

....

....

....

....

....

....

....

....

....

....

....

Love One Another

You who have received so much love share it with others.
Love others the way that God has loved you, with tenderness.

MOTHER TERESA

The reason we can dare to risk loving others
is that "God has for Christ's sake loved us."
Think of it! We are loved eternally, totally, individually,
unreservedly! Nothing can take God's love away.

GLORIA GAITHER

Let Jesus be in your heart,
Eternity in your spirit,
The world under your feet,
The will of God in your actions.
And let the love of God shine forth from you.

CATHERINE OF GENOA

Oh, if we did but love others!
How easily the least thing, the shutting of a door gently,
the walking softly, speaking low, not making a noise,
or the choice of a seat, so as to leave
the most convenient to others,
might become occasions of its exercise.

MÈRE ANGÉLIQUE ARNAULD

Dear friends, since God so loved us, we also ought to love one another....
If we love one another, God lives in us and his love is made complete in us.

1 JOHN 4:11–12 NIV

....

....

....

....

....

....

....

....

....

....

....

....

....

The Love of God

Who shall separate us from the love of Christ?
Shall trouble or hardship or persecution or famine or
nakedness or danger or sword?... No, in all these things we
are more than conquerors through him who loved us.
For I am convinced that neither death nor life, neither angels
nor demons, neither the present nor the future, nor any powers,
neither height nor depth, nor anything else in all creation,
will be able to separate us from the love of God
that is in Christ Jesus our Lord.

ROMANS 8:35, 37–39 NIV

I will be glad and rejoice in your unfailing love,
for you have seen my troubles,
and you care about the anguish of my soul.

PSALM 31:7 NLT

The steadfast love of the LORD never ceases,
his mercies never come to an end; they are new every morning;
great is your faithfulness.

LAMENTATIONS 3:22–23 NRSV

May the Lord direct your hearts into the love of God
and into the steadfastness of Christ.

2 THESSALONIANS 3:5 NASB

Nothing can separate you from His love, absolutely nothing....
God is enough for time, and God is enough for eternity. God is enough!

HANNAH WHITALL SMITH

Always There

We do not need to search for heaven,
over here or over there, in order to find our eternal Father.
In fact, we do not even need to speak out loud,
for though we speak in the smallest whisper
or the most fleeting thought,
He is close enough to hear us.

TERESA OF AVILA

Look for, long for, pray for, and expect special
breaking-through times when
God makes His presence very real, very powerful!
And until they come, dwell in His presence by faith
and gaze upon His beauty.

RAY AND ANNE ORTLUND

God is always present in the temple of your heart...His home.
And when you come in to meet Him there,
you find that it is the one place of deep satisfaction
where every longing is met.

Always be in a state of expectancy,
and see that you leave room
for God to come in as He likes.

OSWALD CHAMBERS

All you need to remember is that God will never let you down;
he'll never let you be pushed past your limit;
he'll always be there to help you come through it.

1 CORINTHIANS 10:13 MSG

....

....

....

....

....

....

....

....

....

....

....

....

Ellie Claire™ Gift & Paper Corp.
Minneapolis, MN 55337
www.ellieclaire.com

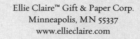
God Is Always with You
© 2011 by Ellie Claire™ Gift & Paper Corp.

ISBN 978-1-60936-244-7

Scripture references are from the following sources: The Holy Bible,
King James Version (KJV). The Holy Bible, New International Version®, NIV®.
Copyright © 1973, 1978, 1984, 2011 by Biblica, Inc.™ Used by permission of
Zondervan. All rights reserved worldwide. The New King James Version (NKJV).
Copyright © 1982 by Thomas Nelson, Inc. Used by permission. The New American
Standard Bible® (NASB), Copyright © 1960, 1962, 1963, 1968, 1971, 1972, 1973,
1975, 1977, 1995 by The Lockman Foundation. Used by permission. The New Revised
Standard Version Bible (NRSV). Copyright 1989, 1995, Division of Christian Education of
the National Council of the Churches of Christ in the United States of America. Used by
permission. The Holy Bible, New Living Translation (NLT), copyright 1996, 2004.
Used by permission of Tyndale House Publishers, Inc., Wheaton, Illinois. *The Message*
(MSG). Copyright © 1993, 1994, 1995, 1996, 2000, 2001, 2002 by Eugene Peterson. Used
by permission of NavPress, Colorado Springs, CO. *The Living Bible* (TLB) © 1971.
Used by permission of Tyndale House Publishers, Inc., Wheaton, Illinois 60189.
All rights reserved.

Excluding Scripture verses, references to men and masculine pronouns
have been replaced with gender-neutral references.

Compiled by Joanie Garborg/Barbara Farmer
Cover and interior designed by David Carlson, Gearbox

Printed in China